It Is More Than the Miracle Question

Deconstructing Solution Focused Therapy

A Volume in
Research, Theory, and Practice Within Academic Affairs

Series Editors

Antione D. Tomlin
Anne Arundel Community College

Sherella Cupid
Louisiana State University

Research, Theory, and Practice Within Academic Affairs

Antione D. Tomlin and Sherella Cupid, Series Editors

*It Is More Than the Miracle Question:
Deconstructing Solution Focused Therapy (2025)*
by Mark Gillen and Blake Mayes

*When We Hear Them:
Attuning Teachers to Language-Diverse Learners (2024)*
edited by Owen Silverman Andrews and Antione D. Tomlin

The Handbook for Aspiring Higher Education Leaders (2024)
edited by Antione D. Tomlinl

Effective Alternative Assessment Practices in Higher Education (2024)
edited by Antione D. Tomlin and Christine M. Nowik

Voices of the Field: DEIA Champions in Higher Education (2023)
edited by Antione D. Tomlin and Sherella Cupid

Black Faculty Do It All: A Moment in the Life of a Blackademic (2023)
edited by Antione D. Tomlin

Don't Forget About the Adjuncts! (2023)
edited by Antione D. Tomlin

It Is More Than the Miracle Question

Deconstructing Solution Focused Therapy

by

Mark Gillen
University of Wisconsin–River Falls

Blake Mayes
Licensed School Counselor in Minnesota

United Kingdom – North America – Japan –
India – Malaysia – China

Emerald Publishing Limited
Emerald Publishing, Floor 5, Northspring, 21-23 Wellington Street, Leeds LS1 4DL

First edition 2025

Copyright © 2025 Susan Mossman Riva.
Published under exclusive licence by Emerald Publishing Limited.

Reprints and permissions service
Contact: www.copyright.com

No part of this book may be reproduced, stored in a retrieval system, transmitted in any form or by any means electronic, mechanical, photocopying, recording or otherwise without either the prior written permission of the publisher or a licence permitting restricted copying issued in the UK by The Copyright Licensing Agency and in the USA by The Copyright Clearance Center. Any opinions expressed in the chapters are those of the authors. Whilst Emerald makes every effort to ensure the quality and accuracy of its content, Emerald makes no representation implied or otherwise, as to the chapters' suitability and application and disclaims any warranties, express or implied, to their use.

British Library Cataloguing in Publication Data
A catalogue record for this book is available from the British Library

ISBN: 978-1-83708-531-6 (Print paperback)
ISBN: 978-1-83708-530-9 (Print hardback)
ISBN: 978-1-83708-532-3 (Ebook)
ISBN: 978-1-83708-533-0 (EPUB)

CONTENTS

Abstract .... *vii*

Prologue .... *ix*

1. Introduction *1*

2. Start at the Beginning *5*
   Section 1: Building and Maintaining a Strong Foundation:
   Micro-Skills Are Vital *5*
   Section 2: It's Just Dancing—Someone Must Lead *7*
   Section 3: Ethical, Developmental, and Cultural Issues *9*
   Section 4: Who Is Your Client? Everyone Is Your Client ... *10*
   Section 5: Failure *11*
   Section 6: Risk and Hope *13*
   Section 7: Be Humble *14*

3. Solution Focused Beliefs That Guide Our Practice *17*
   Section 1: Why Worry About a Belief System at All? *17*
   Section 2: Five Starting Thoughts:
   Bridging Foundational Belief *18*
   Section 3: Marinating *20*
   Section 4: Choose a Theory or It Chooses You *21*
   Section 5: Reframing World View *23*
   Section 6: This Seems Pretty Simplistic—But It Isn't *24*
   Section 7: Get Curious *25*
   Section 8: Assumptions *26*
   Section 9: Enhancing Client Choices *28*

v

Section 10: Resistant Clients.. 29
Section 11: Controversial Thoughts: Don't Work Harder Than
 Your Clients... 30
Section 12: Six More Beliefs to Help Keep You on Track.............. 32

4. **Now What? SFT Techniques** 35

5. **Be Gillen** 39

About the Authors 41

ABSTRACT

The impetus for this book is to help counselors, specifically school counselors, figure out how to utilize a theory, or mindset/belief system, in our everyday work with clients. Dr. Gillen's ideas on how to think like a solution focused counselor were born at the Brief Family Therapy Center (BFTC) in Milwaukee Wisconsin.

This is not a strict academic text, instead this guide offers insights and ideas for utilizing Solution Focused Theory based on training at the Brief Family Therapy Center, years of supervised practice using Solution Focused Theory, readings, research, and decades of training others on how to utilize Solution Focused Therapy (SFT).

Keywords: Counseling, School Counseling, Solution Focused Theory, Clinical Counseling, Brief Family Therapy

PROLOGUE

What I must do is all that concerns me, not what the people think. This rule, equally arduous in actual and in intellectual life, may serve for the whole distinction between greatness and meanness. It is harder, because you will always find those who think they know what is your duty better than you know it. —Ralph Waldo Emerson

The impetus for this book is to help counselors, specifically school counselors, figure out how to utilize a theory, or mindset/belief system, in our everyday work with clients. My ideas on how to think like a solution focused counselor were born at the Brief Family Therapy Center (BFTC) in Milwaukee Wisconsin. Beginning in 1978, Steve DeShazer, Insoo Berg, Eve Lipchik, Elam Nunnally, Jim Derks, and Marilyn Le Court built upon the work of the Mental Research Institute in Palo Alto California. My training at the BFTC began in 1987 and I continue to consult with Eve Lipchik to this day. This is not an academic text, but rather an idea guide based on training at the Brief Family Therapy Center, years of supervised practice using Solution Focused Theory, readings, research, and decades of training others on how to utilize Solution Focused Therapy (SFT).

This book would not be possible without the support and assistance from Blake Mayes, one of my former students who is a current licensed and practicing school counselor in Minnesota. His stories and contributions kept the writing process going. Support and encouragement were also provided by Eve Lipchik who, after all of these years, continues to help me grow in my understanding of solution focused theory. Editing and helping me to focus my writing was thanks to Eve, Blake, Julie Holfetz, and my wife Kate Smith.

It Is More Than the Miracle Question:
Deconstructing Solution Focused Therapy, pp. ix–ix
www.emeraldgrouppublishing.com
Copyright © 2025 by Emerald Publishing
All rights of reproduction in any form reserved.

CHAPTER 1

INTRODUCTION

I like to listen. I have learned a great deal from listening carefully. Most people never listen.—Ernest Hemingway

While this is not an academic textbook, everything you read in this book is based on research, learning, and training that supplements and enhances your understanding and use of Solution Focused Therapy (SFT) as a school counselor. I present on SFT to school counselors and when they take away something that's generally because they are ready to hear it. This book is a one-day professional development training that you can constantly review. It offers a self-paced version of that training. It provides you with the time you need to reflect on the foundation of your work with clients. The more you apply the concepts, the more the chapters and sections will connect. If you are interested in utilizing SFT beliefs and mindsets to better understand and guide your work, then this book is for you. The book also provides foundational guidance to work with your peers on peer-to-peer clinical supervision.

Each chapter includes sections that are brief, focused, and written for easy consumption on a vital SFT issue in your work with clients. I expand on these ideas with research-based practices explained through real-life examples. Each section wraps up with brief *sound bites* or things to remember from the chapter.

So, what will you find in this book?

The premise for learning about SFT is based on the underlying beliefs or mindsets that guide us in our work, not just the techniques. Unlike other

---

It Is More Than the Miracle Question:
Deconstructing Solution Focused Therapy, pp. 1–4
www.emeraldgrouppublishing.com
Copyright © 2025 by Emerald Publishing
All rights of reproduction in any form reserved.

SFT books for school counselors, I first focus on the most important skills, creating relationships, and how relationship-building skills support SFT.

The second chapter is dedicated to reinforcing the skills and considerations necessary to form long-term working relationships with our clients. As you will discover, I consider everyone I work with as a client. That includes students, parents, teachers, staff, administrators, bus drivers, lunch people; in fact, everyone I interact with. This approach lets me use the counseling skills I'm best at with everyone. Also included in this section are reminders about some of the foundational skills because counselors use them every day. These include micro-skills, ethical, developmental, and cultural considerations, as well as basic reminders to stay focused on our clients and what they are looking for, not what we think they need.

Chapter 3 delves deeper into foundational ideas for SFT, outlining six basic concepts vital to using an SFT mindset with clients. This chapter explores the value of being curious while not allowing our assumptions and biases to get in the way of what our clients want to work on. Controversial topics are discussed—like not working harder than our clients, reframing a client's worldview, and the idea that there are no resistant clients, just inflexible counselors. Chapter 3 wraps up with six more foundational concepts to integrate into our daily work.

Looking for techniques? You'll find them in Chapter 4. Practically, any technique can be used once a counselor is comfortable with the underlying foundational beliefs.

Sound bites: Things to remember:

1. This book can be read chronologically or in whatever order strikes your fancy.
2. It is based on research, foundational information, training, and almost 40 years of practice with SFT.
3. Included are three chapters starting with foundational counseling skills, including SFT beliefs and finally potential techniques.

OUTLINE OF CHAPTERS AND SECTIONS

Chapter 2: Start at the Beginning

The sections in this chapter focus on the primary skills that all counselors use to form a relationship with their clients. Relationship building is the cornerstone of our work in schools and without the ability to listen, empathize, and connect with clients, the application of SFT beliefs is less effective.

Section 1: Building and Maintaining a Strong Foundation
Section 2: Micro-Skills Are Vital
Section 3: It's Just Dancing—Someone Must Lead
Section 4: Ethical, Developmental, and Cultural Issues
Section 5: Who Is Your Client? Everyone Is Your Client
Section 6: Failure
Section 7: Risk and Hope
Section 8: Be Humble

Chapter 3: Solution Focused Beliefs That Guide Our Practice

The sections in this chapter explore specific solution focused theoretical beliefs that guide how counselors interact with clients. The goal is to explore theoretical underpinnings using everyday terminology. Counselors who begin with a sound understanding of the theory can use that knowledge to lead naturally into application and technique.

Section 1: Why Worry About A Belief System at All?
Section 2: Six Basic Thoughts: Bridging Foundational Beliefs.

1. We are facilitators—not fixers.
2. The past is important but not defining.
3. Remember to recognize small successes.
4. There are often multiple clients.
5. Once a client knows we are on their side, make suggestions through common ground.
6. Look for the simplest answer that fits (for your client).

Section 3: Marinating
Section 4: Reframing Worldview
Section 5: This Seems Pretty Simplistic—But It Isn't
Section 6: Get Curious
Section 7: Assumptions
Section 8: Enhancing Client Choices: One Thing at a Time
Section 9: Resistant Clients
Section 10: Don't Work Harder Than Your Client
Section 11: Six More Beliefs to Help Keep You on Track

1. Small change leads to bigger change.
2. Change in one part of the system leads to chaos.
3. Counselors do not have the power or knowledge to change clients.
4. No two situations are exactly alike.
5. No situation is all negative.
6. Success is negotiable.

Chapter 4: Now What? SFT Techniques

The sections in this chapter offer some specific solution focused techniques for school counselors as well as other techniques that may not be considered solution focused.

Slow down
Miracle Question
Positive blame
Flag the minefield
Scaling questions
Caring confrontation

CHAPTER 2

START AT THE BEGINNING

You can only help people if you yourself have a strong foundation to draw from.
—Richard Branson

SECTION 1: BUILDING AND MAINTAINING A STRONG FOUNDATION: MICRO-SKILLS ARE VITAL

What Is This Section About and How Does It Connect With SFT?

Working with clients requires creating a solid foundation. Before we begin to consider using any theory, micro-skills establish a relationship with a client. Some of the essential micro-skill competencies include non-verbal interactions, restatement of content, reflections of feelings, common ground techniques with clients, and continuity from opening to closing. Once you have a relationship established, you can then begin to consider how to utilize solution focused beliefs or mindsets with clients.

Discussion

When training counselors on the solution focused mindset, I often begin with a video interview with Eve Lipchik, one of the co-founders of SFT, on the most important things to remember when learning and using SFT. The first is to create a relationship with your client. It sounds simple enough,

---

It Is More Than the Miracle Question:
Deconstructing Solution Focused Therapy, pp. 5–16
www.emeraldgrouppublishing.com
Copyright © 2025 by Emerald Publishing
All rights of reproduction in any form reserved.

but remembering to use the basic skills is one of the cornerstones of a good working relationship. If you don't have good relationship-building skills, you will never progress to integrating a theory, like SFT, because you and your client are not on the same pathway.

Foundational skills begin with non-verbal listening skills. Open body positioning, also known as the SOLER position (sitting upright, open posture, lean in, eye contact, relax) and "yes sets" (nodding your head) lay the foundation and are skills you use every time you listen to clients. Other vital listening skills include restating content, reflecting feelings, and using short, focused questions to help you understand the client's goals. Restating content includes listening carefully to the client's story and then paraphrasing what you have heard. For example, I encourage counselors to use the phrase, "What I hear you saying is…," and then add the paraphrase. This restatement does three things, (1) allows the client to know that you are listening, (2) reflects back to the client their ideas through your lens, and (3) helps the client to determine if this is the story they want to use. Counselors do not need to get the paraphrase correct every time. Listening is hard work and sometimes you miss information, or clients don't share the whole story. However, when you miss something, it offers clients the ability to correct us. This is a beautiful moment because the counselor lets the client know that they are working hard to listen and understand, but are not infallible. Restatements of content can also encourage clients to broaden their story by providing more context.

When you reflect a client's feelings back to them, there can also be positive consequences. In this case, the opening line is, "Sounds like you are feeling…." and then you insert a feeling. Like the restatement of content, it does not have to be the correct feeling, just close, because if the feeling isn't right, clients will correct us. We are not the experts on what our clients are feeling. They are. While restating content broadens the conversation, reflecting a feeling deepens the conversation. Feelings can represent a lot of baggage for clients, so reflecting a feeling is vital, but should be used judiciously. I also encourage counselors to not combine a feeling and content into one response. It creates a dichotomy for clients. Are you asking them to expand their story or deepen their story?

Focused questions can also help a client to continue telling their story. A favorite response of mine is, "Tell me more," and I especially like it for two reasons. I am not interjecting myself into the client's conversation for very long and when I end the statement, it is not a question. By using the word "more" the client can go in any direction they choose. If, instead, I end the statement with "Tell me more about the interaction with your sister," then I drive the client to a topic I am interested in. While this may be the direction the client is going, it is not uncommon that clients will change directions to topics that have not yet come up, and that they truly want to talk about.

Another foundational skill is common ground. Creating common ground with a client is something I encourage counselors to use, especially when they hear a client talking about a topic as if they are the only person going through a particular issue. For example, I work with a lot of school-age children and often they say they are struggling to make friends. A common ground statement includes an opening statement and a type of paraphrase that provides support for their situation and lets them know that they are not the only ones dealing with this issue; in fact, others have dealt with it successfully. In the case of friendship, a common ground statement might be "I have worked with a lot of other third graders who have told me that making friends is hard work and sometimes doesn't always go as they hoped or planned." My third-grade clients are much more likely to listen to what other third-graders have told me and how they have dealt with the issue than what I think they ought to do. After all, what does some grown-up know about the world of a third-grader?

Foundational skills are used constantly and provide the framework to add the theoretical beliefs, in the case of this book, solution focused counseling.

Sound Bites: Things to Remember From This Section

1. Connecting with clients is vital to create a working relationship.
2. Clients know we are listening when we use foundational skills, including purposeful non-verbal communication, like open posture and "yes sets."
3. We reinforce our relationship with clients when we use verbal communication skills like restating content, reflecting feelings, using minimal questions, and creating common ground. Each of these skills reinforces that the client is the primary focus, and the session depends upon them.

SECTION 2: IT'S JUST DANCING—SOMEONE MUST LEAD

Sometimes you lead, sometimes you follow. Don't worry about what you don't know. Life is a dance; you learn as you go. —John Michael Montgomery

What Is This Section About and How Does It Connect With SFT?

Working with clients is like dancing. The client leads and the counselor must determine the client's style and tempo of the dance. Then, like any good partner, the counselor changes the dance ever so slightly to shift or reframe the client's view of the world. SFT is based upon the client being the expert on themselves.

Discussion

The dance analogy is especially germane because when two people are doing the same dance, it's easier to work together. The challenge is, who's leading? Adept and nimble counselors shift from their preferred dance to determine what dance the client is doing. They do this by utilizing foundational micro-skills to learn the dance steps, tempo, and music that the client hears. Counselors know that they are getting closer to the client's dance when the client engages and explores issues that are important to them.

The most important skill to help counselors learn their client's dance is to slow down. Counselors need to be purposeful as they quickly shuffle ideas, listen, and process information. In Eve Lipchik's (2002) book *Beyond Technique in Solution Focused Therapy* she called this parallel thinking. Parallel thinking includes multi-level processing; the ability to listen to the client while considering how to take the next steps to stay with the client.

As discussed in the previous section, a vital skill is to be well-versed in basic micro-skills. Restating what the client is saying, reflecting on what they might be feeling, listening, and hearing what clients are saying all leads to a more robust relationship with the client. This deeper relationship provides the client with an opportunity to explore their issues more fully.

Some moments require that you change the pace of the dance and cognitive dissonance can be key. A client may say something that conflicts with their actions, creating dissonance. At those moments, I stop the dance and confront the shift. I am curious about what the client has shared. I need to provide opportunities for clients to consider what I have said and respond. Then the dance continues, but with a slightly different tempo.

One of the most common counselor speed bumps is insisting that the client dance to your tune instead of taking the time and effort to learn the client's dance. Pushing ahead too quickly, making assumptions about clients, and not being in the moment with a client all lead to a diminished connection and relationship. A tip-off for counselors that they are relying too much on their dance is when they view the clients as resistant.

A Brief Story

A few years ago my wife and I took ballroom dance lessons. Each week, we would join about a dozen other people to go over basic dance steps and attempt to connect them with the music. My wife is a musician by training, so she quickly grasped the connection between step patterns and musical tempo. On the other hand, I found that while I could memorize the step patterns, I struggled to make the leap, connecting them with the tempo of the music. At one point near our final lesson, we were dancing together when my wife said to me, "You know there is music that goes with the steps?" I did. But finding the connection was difficult. It was then that I realized that learning to dance with music is just like working with clients. They know their dance steps and their music. I know neither. However, I know that by building a relationship with clients, and appropriately using micro-skills, I can follow their lead.

Sound Bites: Things to Remember About This Section

1. The client is doing a dance and we need to adjust our dance to follow their lead. To do this we listen closely, really listen, to what they are saying verbally and non-verbally.
2. When they share something that doesn't add up, for instance, when they say one thing but are doing something else, then we explore with the client if they are okay with those choices.

SECTION 3: ETHICAL, DEVELOPMENTAL, AND CULTURAL ISSUES

The first step in the evolution of ethics is a sense of solidarity with other humans.
—Albert Schweitzer

What Is This Section About and How Does It Connect With SFT?

These three issues are vital when working with clients. If you forget any of these, you could miss something that plays an integral role in understanding a client.

Discussion

Let's start with ethical issues. While ethical issues may seem straightforward and clear because there are professional ethical codes and abundant training to maintain licensure, defining ethical dilemmas and how to approach them can be complex. There are several ethical decision-making models to consider, but in the heat of the moment, I recommend an abbreviated ethical decision-making model that has three straightforward parts. When you've determined a response you'll use with a client, is it one that you would: (1) declare standing on a table, (2) in a well-lit room filled with your peers and (3) proudly proclaim out loud? If not, you may be facing an ethical issue that requires a more complex evaluation model.

What are you really good at? You may be really good at a sport, music, or academics. However, competency is developmental and resides along a continuum. We tend to consider developmental issues using a model that focuses only on the age and stage of the client. For example, often we assume all third graders tend to think this way or act one way. This information may be based on well-researched developmental theories. However, more complex developmental issues that influence how a client sees and responds to the world will vary with each client.

Similar to developmental issues, cultural issues or life experiences are often considered solely in the context of racial and ethnic identity. Cultural life experiences are much more robust and include everything that has influenced a client and helped them get to where they are today. Listening carefully to the life experiences of a client and attempting to understand how this impacts their choices is a vital part of counseling. It's essential to remember that while we have knowledge and training in the areas of ethical, cultural, and developmental issues, the client is the one who will help us to understand their life experiences.

Sound Bites: Things to Remember About This Section

1. As you are creating a relationship with your client, it is vital to keep in mind the three foundational issues—cultural or life experience issues, developmental issues, and ethical issues.
2. Keep in mind that at any moment you may become embroiled in an ethical decision-making situation, so have a plan on how to evaluate your decisions.
3. Developmental issues are unique to each individual and using exceptional listening skills helps us to understand where our client is on a continuum.
4. Listen for cultural life experiences and let your client guide you in understanding who they are.

SECTION 4: WHO IS YOUR CLIENT?

Who looks outside dreams; who looks inside awakes. —Carl Jung

What Is This Section About and How Does It Connect With SFT?

A key component for becoming fully marinated as a solution focused counselor is to shift your worldview. As you become more and more immersed in the theory, you may find that your professional worldview and your personal worldview overlap. This chapter suggests that everyone you come into contact with as a counselor is your client, including your students and all adults in their lives. We will explore the unique skills that a school counselor brings into the school system along with solution focused belief systems.

Discussion

One of the more challenging mindsets I use is the idea that everyone I interact with as a school counselor is my client. A school counselor's unique skill set should not be defined by the assignments they're given, but by the relationship-building and counseling training they bring into the school environment. It's important to remember that others in the school system have not received this training. One of the primary focuses of our unique skill set involves creating relationships with people and then allowing them to find ways to solve their problems.

A Brief Story

After my first year of grad school, I was working in summer programming for a local school district. One of my co-workers was a recent high school graduate. Over time, as we built a relationship, he began to open up to me about some of his experiences in the past and how he was both excited and scared about taking the next step by attending college and moving away from home in the fall. During one of our conversations, I used some of my new my counseling skills and his positive response startled me. I remember thinking that I didn't do anything special, I merely wanted to learn a little bit more about him and as we talked, I let him lead the way.

When we consider everyone we come in contact with professionally as a client, our skills become authentic to who we are and how we interact with the world around us.

Sound Bites: Things to Remember About This Section

1. Everyone is our client.
2. Be consistent in our interactions with others, allowing others to understand what we do and what we will not do.

SECTION 5: FAILURE

Success is not final; failure is not fatal: It is the courage to continue that counts.
—Winston S. Churchill

What Is This Section About and How Does It Connect With SFT?

In this section, we explore the vital role that failure plays in our work. We can see failure as an inability to connect with clients, or to understand what clients are looking for. However, failure in counseling relationships can provide opportunities to learn and refine our skills. Seen in this light, failures with clients can provide valuable chances to expand our counseling competencies.

Discussion

Counselors don't always get it right; it's inevitable to err. However, self-reflection is crucial to determine if something could've been done differently or if the client got what they needed. As someone who likes to process things verbally, I have found it helpful to cultivate relationships with others in the counseling profession, including the others in my building. Consulting is an essential component of development. In graduate school, I was required to journal at least once a week during internships and I continue to integrate this practice into my career as a method for evaluating, practicing, and maintaining a growth-focused mindset that leads to better outcomes for both clients and the counselor. Without reflecting upon difficult moments, I myself fall into bad counseling habits without taking the opportunity to correct them.

Recently, I was talking to one of my colleagues and the conversation didn't go very well. I then went into a meeting with one of my students, but I found myself focusing more on the previous conversation and had a hard time moving on from my earlier frustration. I continued to consider the earlier conversation with my colleague and what I could've done differently. At times, my student almost had to do my job for me by asking me for responses. Eventually, I was able to fully engage in the conversation but left disappointed that I hadn't fully engaged in the conversation with my student.

There have been moments when I wasn't sure what a client required. Those are the times when I rely on my client to guide me. An example of this happened when a student I had worked with previously walked in with the typical question: "Are you busy?" Before I could answer, she started talking about some of the things that were bothering her. Without taking a breath, she blazed through many years of struggling with self-image and examining where some of those issues came from. I found myself relying on foundational counseling skills and staying attuned to the twists and turns of her thoughts. When the bell rang, I looked up at the clock and couldn't believe that she had been talking for more than 45 minutes. I hadn't said a word. I had simply used "yes sets" by nodding my head and saying "mmhmm" over and over again. I felt like a complete failure. I never found a way to get a word in and didn't feel like I did anything helpful. However, when she finished talking, she said "Wow, thank you so much for talking with me, this was so, so helpful," and walked out. I was stunned.

Both of these examples highlight the difference between feeling like a failure as a school counselor and actually failing as a counselor. In the first example, I did not bring my "A game" to the conversation with my student. I was distracted and wasn't able to mute my internal monologue to truly engage with my student. In the second example, I used my foundational counseling skills to listen while allowing the client to lead. The client just needed to feel heard, and she didn't need me to "do" anything except use the relationship-building and listening skills we are good at as counselors.

Sound Bites: Things To Remember From This Section

1. Failure happens. Counselors must fail to learn and grow professionally.
2. Clients help us to grow professionally by working with us to learn about working with people and applying our foundational skills and theoretical mindsets.

SECTION 6: RISK AND HOPE

There are risks and costs to action. But they are far less than the long-range risks of comfortable inaction. —John F. Kennedy

What Is This Section About and How Does It Connect With SFT?

Each time we meet with a client, they are constantly making decisions on how much risk they're willing to endure. This consideration of potential risk is weighed against the amount of hope that they may have in producing a change. While it may seem that risk and hope are two different issues, they go hand-in-hand.

A BRIEF STORY

Regardless of how a student ends up at our door, they are taking a risk talking to their counselor. The mere act of showing up to see us is change, and change is risky. As humans, we are typically most comfortable with the status quo, even if we don't love everything about our situation. Moving towards change, even if it's a small move, can be threatening. However, clients don't end up with a school counselor because of the risk. Their hope for something better is what gets them there.

Our vision of our reality is based on previous experiences. Many times, a student has conflicting visions of how they would like things to be, and that can affect their ideas of hope and reality. Say it's the end of the semester and a student has a very low grade but wants to get an A. This may not be possible now, but at this moment we can ask, "I know you want an A, but you have an F and there's a week left in the semester. What can you live with?" You leave the door open allowing the student to consider their goals, including how much risk and change they are willing to take, and engaging them to envision the steps to get to where they want to go.

Hope and risk influence client actions. There's hope that something will be different, but it is also a risk. Change doesn't always lead to something better; it leads to something different. Therefore, deciding to change means uncertainty, including risk and hope.

Sound Bites: Things to Remember From This Section

1. Risk and hope are two sides of the same coin. Clients take risks with the hope that things will be different.

SECTION 7: BE HUMBLE

It's hard to be humble when you're perfect in every way. —Mac Davis

What Is This Section About and How Does It Connect With SFT?

This section, the final in this chapter, is a reminder that as counselors we are just one of many contacts clients utilize to work with on their issues. Maintaining a humble attitude helps counselors stay in the moment and allows the client to lead. This core belief reinforces SFT theory and reminds counselors that clients know themselves better than counselors ever will.

A Brief Story

A teacher approaches you with a concern about one of their students, again. You have heard this story many times from this teacher. As they continue to share the latest version of events, you hear them less and less. Your internal voice begins to spin up with a myriad of "appropriate" responses and advice that you are sure will respond to this situation. You can't wait for them to stop talking so you can share your ideas that are certain to make this all better. Then, they stop talking and say that they just wanted to run this idea by you and will keep thinking about it. They end with, "Thanks for listening."

You are stunned. You didn't get to share your magnificent knowledge, but you also didn't really hear what they were saying. That isn't how counseling is supposed to work. Clients come to see the school counselor to share their innermost issues and are looking for your input to change the trajectory of their lives. Doesn't that client know you have a master's degree in counseling?

You have forgotten a few vital rules for working with clients from a SFT perspective.

- Graduate degrees don't guarantee that we know everything about a client.
- What we know about a client is what we learn from them. Clients lead the session and we need to be humble enough to be in the moment with them.

In this case, we didn't learn anything. When the teacher needed us to listen, we were simply hearing them make mouth noises. We forgot that client's issues don't magically appear the moment they begin talking with us. Clients spend a lot of time thinking through issues before they talk with us and once they leave our meeting, they continue to contemplate ideas and chat with others until finally they either do something or decide not to do anything. We are just one person in what may be a long line of "helpers" for a client.

However, there is something important that we do differently for our clients. As discussed in the section on microskills, we actively listen to our clients, not just hear their mouth noise. We must tamp down our own thoughts and listen carefully to our clients. They may just want to talk about things. They may not need a solution—yet. Or they may want to do something different - now. Either way, they have chosen us as one of the people they talk to and we owe them our best counseling skills.

Ultimately, this mindset requires humility. Our egos must be strong enough to deal with the fact that clients may not recognize how competent we are at utilizing advanced theoretical counseling skills. They just want someone to listen.

A Brief Story

Each day before going to work, I choose a coffee cup that seems appropriate for the day. My wife and I have a shelf full of cups from our travels.

Many days I choose a specific cup given to me by a professional board while I was its president. I got the cup as a thank-you for reviewing what seemed like 5,000 high school scholarship applications. It was probably only 50 applications, but I was delighted with the gift. However, when I opened the box, I was surprised to find that my name had been misspelled. I was the president! How could this happen? They offered to take the cup back, however; I keep it to remind myself that no matter how big a deal we think we are, someone may still not spell our name correctly. Be humble. Take it in stride. It isn't malicious. If your ego can't stand a little bruising, then working with clients may not be for you.

Sound Bites: Things to Remember From This Section

1. You are just one of many contacts for clients. They begin to consider issues long before meeting with you and will continue to think about the issue long after they meet with you.
2. Counselors are not the center of the client's universe.
3. Steve deShazer, co-founder of Solution Focused Theory, wrote that understanding a client is a lot like opening a lock. You don't need a key for every lock if you understand how locks work. To accomplish this by utilizing SFT a school counselor must be humble, or you will spend all your client time trying out new keys instead of listening carefully to understand how your client's lock works.

REFERENCE

Lipchik, E. (2002). *Beyond technique in solution focused therapy.* Guilford Press.

CHAPTER 3

SOLUTION FOCUSED BELIEFS THAT GUIDE OUR PRACTICE

It is the repetition of affirmations that leads to a belief. Once that belief becomes a deep conviction then things begin to happen. —Muhammad Ali

SECTION 1: WHY WORRY ABOUT A BELIEF SYSTEM AT ALL?

What Is This Section About and How Does It Connect With SFT?

This section covers a brief introduction to why a Solution Focused Theory (SFT) belief system can enhance and strengthen your work with clients. How can this approach make a difference? Of course, you want to always utilize skills that build relationships with your clients. However, beyond this, it's important to investigate theories and find one that fits for you. We hope that you choose SFT, but whatever theory you choose, you want to dive deep into learning, training, and practicing with supervision.

Why? Primarily because working with clients is complicated and while listening to and supporting your clients, you will be pushed to your limit. When you have a theory that you are well grounded in, you possess a pathway to work and stay engaged. When we don't have a theory guiding our actions, we make things up, and that is when we get into trouble.

It Is More Than the Miracle Question:
Deconstructing Solution Focused Therapy, pp. 17–34
www.emeraldgrouppublishing.com
Copyright © 2025 by Emerald Publishing
All rights of reproduction in any form reserved.

Sound Bites: Things to Remember From This Section

1. Choose a theory that works for you and your clients. Then immerse yourself in learning and practicing with support.

SECTION 2: FIVE STARTING THOUGHTS: BRIDGING FOUNDATIONAL BELIEFS

Whatever good things we build end up building us. —Jim Rohn

What Is This Section About and How Does It Connect With SFT?

In this section, we look at five specific foundational beliefs, or mindsets to guide school counselors in their work with clients and make the bridge between foundational relationship-building skills to SFT beliefs.

1. **We are facilitators—not fixers.**

One of the most common misconceptions regarding SFT is that the counselor is responsible for coming up with answers for the client. That's not our job, nor are we smart enough about our clients to come up with ideas that will work for them. However, we do know who has the experiences and ideas that could work: clients themselves.

2. **The past is important but not defining.**

Clients often want to spend time talking about past events that have influenced their lives, and the associated problems. While the problems are important to understand, it is also vital to focus on times when the problem is not occurring to know how a client has managed to work through previous challenges. When we focus solely on the problem, any thought about how the client would like things to change, or how they envision their life without the problem, is ignored.

3. **Remember to recognize small successes.**

As counselors, it's important to listen for changes in behavior. Any small change related to the problem is important while remembering that a change in behavior does not always mean it's for the better. Sometimes things get worse, and then clients have a choice; whether they can live with the issues or want to choose to do something different. Listening carefully and interrupting the client's "dance" to clarify small successes or changes, is an important skill to utilize.

4. **There are often multiple clients.**

There is always an identified client. Usually, it is the primary person you are working with. However, we often have a constellation of clients. For example, in schools, teachers, administrators, and other adults often approach counselors to talk about an identified client. A typical conversation goes something like this: "I really need you to talk with Jane about her homework. I have tried everything to get her to turn in her work, and she still refuses. I know she is capable of completing the work successfully, but maybe you can talk to her and get her to turn in her past assignments?"

In addition to Jane, the teacher is now also a client and we can use our counseling skills with both clients. As always, we begin to create a relationship by listening carefully and exploring what would be most helpful in the moment. A note of caution. When you meet with an identified client/student who is missing assignments and after talking with you, they begin to turn in their homework; you become a miracle worker providing some magical skill that is not available to others. It may seem attractive to work miracles, but it's far more valuable for you to look for times when the student turns in their homework without any intervention. You can then explore with the teacher how they have helped make that happen with the student. This extremely effective technique is called positive blame. For more information on techniques, check out Chapter 4.

5. **Look for the simplest answer that fits (for your client).**

The law of Ockham's razor, lex parsimoniae or the law of parsimony, is a problem-solving principle that suggests that when presented with competing hypothetical answers to a problem, one should select the one that makes the fewest assumptions. For example, when you hear hoofbeats, you think horses, not zebras. Many ideas may fit, but one of the statements that I make most often with clients is, "I know you love this idea. Which one can you live with?" I also say, "What would be most helpful now?" Each of these statements focuses a client on the simplest response.

Sound Bites: Things to Remember From This Section

1. Keep foundational ideas uppermost in your mind when working with clients.
2. Do not overcomplicate your work.

SECTION 3: MARINATING

The mind is like tofu, it tastes like whatever you marinate it in. —Sylvia Boorstein

What Is This Section About and How Does It Connect With SFT?

Learning a new theory and applying a new theory are two different issues. Counselors can intellectually absorb the theory, but applying it requires a mindset that comes with time, patience, and practice to guide our work with clients. Think of this as marinating in a theory. Since you are reading this book, I hope that you're interested in learning and applying SFT; however, marinating applies to any theory. To purposefully apply a theory, you need to be steeped in the beliefs, not just the techniques.

A Brief Story

Very early in my career, I thought that being a counselor was the easiest job in the world. I actually told a friend, "I just ask a question and they talk." Thirty-five years after making that comment, I understand how foolish and short-sighted I was. Now I am "well-marinated" in a theory and think about my work with clients very differently while realizing that my approach continues to develop.

Recently, I was giving a presentation at a counseling conference on utilizing SFT with clients, primarily in schools. I started with a picture of a jar of pickles. "How do you make pickles?" I asked the audience. A few brave souls shout out, "You get cucumbers," "Put them in a jar," "Cover them with brine."

At that point I asked, "And if you open up the jar of pickles too soon what do you get?"

The answer is that you get salty cucumbers. The secret to making pickles is adequate time to marinate. Marinating is what counselors need to become adept at using a counseling theory. It is not enough just to read about it in a book, take a class, attend a presentation, or try out a few techniques. You must give yourself enough time with the theory so that your clients can help you learn how to apply your theory of choice.

Sound Bites: Things to Remember From This Section

1. Be patient with yourself as you marinate in a theory.
2. Get support and clinical supervision as you continue to grow in your theoretical knowledge.

3. Learning is never-ending. The best teachers are your clients who will provide you with numerous opportunities to learn.

SECTION 4: CHOOSE A THEORY OR IT CHOOSES YOU

The greatest weapon against stress is our ability to choose one thought over another. —William James

What Is This Section About and How Does It Connect With SFT?

Every time I present on SFT, I get two questions.

1. Do you use any other theory besides SFT?
2. Does SFT work for all clients?

The answers are no and yes, respectively. To be clear, I use relationship-building skills that are based on Carl Rogers' work. I use techniques from other theories, but my belief about how I think about clients is based solely on SFT. However, this doesn't mean SFT will work for you. As you know from reading this book, you need enough time with a theory to fully integrate the beliefs into your work with clients. Once you get to this point, you discover that you'll never know everything about the theory or how to use it, primarily because clients are complicated and theories are as well. I hope that you choose to utilize SFT for your professional career, but if not, then find a theory that works for you and dive in.

A Brief Story

I was trained as a Rogerian counselor. If you attended a public university in Wisconsin in the 1970s and 1980s, you were trained in Rogers' person-centered theory. It was the gold standard. The practical training was similar to today's experiences, except that then, we used actual tape machines and cameras as big as suitcases. I understood the basics and believed I was applying the theory thoughtfully and with purpose. Instead, I was applying techniques and hoping the theory would magically appear.

As a nascent school counselor, then an adventure therapy counselor, and finally a community counselor, I found that it was difficult to apply Rogerian theory purposefully with my clientele. I moved on to reality theory, even attending a training by William Glasser. It was helpful, but again I was failing to understand the theory or how to apply it to clients.

Instead, I learned a few techniques and tried to apply them. When the techniques didn't work, I blamed the theory.

In 1987, I was hired by an adventure and group-based day treatment program for 11–14-year-old boys and girls already in the justice system. The first day I met my group for activities, the clients were literally running around the room, jumping up on the walls, and throwing food at each other. One of the clients looked at me as I wondered what I had gotten myself into and said, "Mark, I bet this isn't what you expected?"

Indeed, it wasn't. My cursory understanding of theory wasn't going to help me now. While I struggled with interactions and counseling skills, my program director threw me a lifeline. He had attended a training at the Brief Family Therapy Center in Milwaukee and decided that the lead counselor and I should attend a similar training once a month for six months. I was all for it. A paid day to sit through some training, and not have to work with 11–14-year-olds in the justice system, seemed like a dream.

Unfortunately, I still did not understand what I was missing; a mindset that would help me work with clients and the time to practice and understand how to use that mindset appropriately. However, as the months went by, I realized that something new was happening to me and my work. I began to appreciate how the co-founders of SFT Steve DeShazer, Insoo Berg, and my direct supervisor, Eve Lipchik, connected with clients and their issues by utilizing a theory. Like my mentors, I began to understand and apply a model based on theoretical beliefs rather than techniques.

I continued work in this day treatment center for the next decade, supported by my peers and monthly supervision with Eve Lipchik. She would review tapes of our group, family, and individual counseling and, as a team of three, we discussed how to employ SFT every day. We solidified our work by writing a pamphlet in an attempt to understand what we were doing with clients. We presented at conferences and discussed our work with our counseling peers. What we really were doing during those 10 years was marinating in the theory so that we could apply the mindset to our work with our specific clientele.

Fast forward to today; I am a counselor educator with almost two decades of experience training others in theory and practice. It might seem that I am well-marinated, yet my understanding and application of SFT work continues to develop while working with clients and counseling students. Each year I find new ideas that are solution focused and integrate them into my mindset. Presenting to school counselors and working with them on SFT is one of the most important ways that my marinating continues. However, I am constantly reminded that everyone is somewhere along the learning curve and it's important to discuss theory based on where students and counselors are, not where I am. I was reminded of this a few years ago while presenting at a state conference of school counselors and students.

After the presentation, I was eating lunch at a table with some people who attended my session. I asked, "What is something I talked about that was a real takeaway for you?" Without missing a beat one of the people said, "I never knew how you made pickles!" Fair enough, not what I was hoping for, but it was where the student needed to start.

Sound Bites: Things To Remember From This Section

1. Be "ready" to learn about and utilize a theory.
2. Marinating requires purposefully exploring, understanding, and applying comprehensive knowledge upon which you build your techniques and client interactions.
3. Find a theory that fits your style and clientele. Time and patience are two requisites. You will need to take a class, read a book, or participate in a professional development training and continue to do so over time.
4. Central to the marinating process—you can't do this alone. Collaborate, consult, and find other school counselors to form a learning community.
5. Solidify your knowledge—participate in conference presentations, professional development, write, and share.
6. Be willing to move on from your "chosen" theory if it doesn't connect for you or your clientele. This isn't a sign of failure, but a willingness to look at your choices and then move in a new direction.

SECTION 5: REFRAMING WORLD VIEW

Learning life's lessons is not about making your life perfect, but about seeing life as it is meant to be. —Elisabeth Kubler-Ross

What Is This Section About and How Does It Connect With SFT?

A client's view of their world can be challenged through reframing. This approach offers a client an opportunity to hear feedback on their issue from a different perspective. Then they can choose to keep doing what they are doing or make changes for a new outcome.

A Brief Story

I was observing an intern working with a student who spent much of fifteen minutes talking about how they didn't like school, had difficulty completing homework, and suffered from a sense that they didn't belong. To their credit, the intern explored these concerns with the client, noting that they had a B average in school and had recently turned in all of their assignments. The intern said, "I am curious how that happened?"

"I just did the work and turned it in," stated the student.

"Hmm, sounds like that worked for you. Would you be willing to do more of that?" the intern said.

"Probably," the student responded.

"You know the other thing I am curious about is that I see you in the hallways talking with other students, you sit with people at lunch and talk with them. The same goes for getting on the bus. As you are waiting for your bus I see you spending time with many of these same students, even sitting with them as you load onto the bus," the intern continued.

"Sure, I have some friends," the student said.

As the exchange was drawing to a close, the student said they needed to get back to class and ended by saying, "Thanks for letting me talk. You know I just can't talk about these things with any adult." And out they went.

Afterward, we reviewed what had happened, especially how the intern had not fallen for the student's initial conclusion that nothing was good by responding that things were not as bad as they seemed. Instead, the intern focused on times when the problems were not occurring. Doing some homework, which included observing the student's actions and checking their records, the intern was able to reframe the problem from something constant to something occasional. Then we discussed the client's final statement about not being able to talk to adults. This presented one more excellent opportunity to reframe the problem by noting that the intern was an adult and that the client had just spent a lot of time and energy interacting with an adult regarding their concerns. In other words, reframing the issue.

Sound Bites: Things to Remember From This Section

1. A client's view of their world can be challenged through reframing.
2. Reframe the problem from an all-the-time problem to a sometimes problematic situation.
3. Do not fall into the trap that nothing is good.
4. Explore when the problem is not occurring and what the client has done to achieve that.

SECTION 6: THIS SEEMS PRETTY SIMPLISTIC—BUT IT ISN'T

Everything should be made as simple as possible, but not simpler. —Albert Einstein

WHAT IS THIS SECTION ABOUT AND HOW DOES IT CONNECT WITH SFT?

While some of the issues and concepts we have discussed may seem simple, applying them is difficult and requires constant attention and review.

A Brief Story

When presenting on SFT, I often use a video interview I conducted with Eve Lipchik where we discuss aspects of the therapeutic model that someone starting out should keep in mind. Eve emphasizes going slowly because one of the things that most counselors new to SFT tend to do is provide a solution for the client, instead of exploring a client's issue and what they're doing to keep it in check when it's not posing an immediate problem. Lipchik talks about listening to clients with this advice: "I know you think you're listening, but you need to really listen to what the client is saying."

Our discussion then turns to how SFT has been touted as a quick, or brief therapy, but in reality, it's neither brief nor easy. It requires that you create a relationship with your client by listening closely and being curious about what they want to talk about, not what you are interested in, or your assumption of what they want to talk about. All of this takes time and skill, but in the end, clients are encouraged by their ability to make changes and utilize solutions that work for them in the long term. The best outcome for me, as a counselor, is to have clients walk away thinking, "Sure, Gillen helped some, but really I solved that on my own."

Sound Bites: Things to Remember From This Section

1. Go slowly. Slow yourself down by relying upon the client to guide you.
2. Use your active listening skills.
3. Do not assume you are smarter about the client than they are about themselves.

SECTION 7: GET CURIOUS

If you don't know anything you pay attention to the unusual. —Robert Parker

What Is This Section About and How Does It Connect With SFT?

Curiosity is vital to understanding what a client would like to focus on and what they're willing to do. What does a client want to talk about? This knowledge is vital. Unfortunately, we get in our own way if we are unwilling to listen, really listen, to what our clients are saying to determine what would be helpful to them. We stumble professionally when we leap to conclusions about what they're saying and what they want to do. When a student starts talking about not being able to get their work turned in, we might immediately begin thinking about ways to help them solve this issue. We may even find ourselves coming up with plans for them. Instead, we need to remain curious, and not judgemental about what clients are telling us.

A Brief Story

A teacher catches a counselor in the hallway and shares their concern about a student who continues to not turn in any work. The teacher wants the counselor involved, saying, "I've tried everything I know how to do and nothing, absolutely nothing is working and this just can't go on." Now is the time to employ counseling skills, taking a few minutes to listen, engage, and allow the teacher and student to share what would be helpful to them. This is not about what we can help them with. We need to be curious about what a client wants to explore. Clients should drive the focus and help determine the outcomes with support and guidance from the counselor.

Sound Bites: Things to Remember From This Section

1. A vital component in working with clients is to be curious about what they want to explore, not what you are most interested in.

SECTION 8: ASSUMPTIONS

Begin challenging your own assumptions. Your assumptions are your windows on the world. Scrub them off every once in a while, or the light won't come in.
—*Alan Alda*

What Is This Section About and How Does It Connect With SFT?

We are constantly making assumptions about other people and the situations we find ourselves in. We go through our days making snap judgments and decisions. Instead of spending a great deal of time trying to change how we think about things, it is more productive to work to recognize as many assumptions as possible. In this section, we will examine the process of identifying assumptions and how to approach our thinking patterns as a school counselor who uses SFT.

A Brief Story

During solution focused training, I ask participants to look at a picture of an oddly painted crooked white line on a street that's supposed to indicate a bike lane. For 40 feet, the jagged line goes all over the place. However, there's also a straight line where clearly the worker repainted the line as originally intended. Perhaps someday, they'll remove the unappealing jagged line, but the SFT issue that we want to consider is how did they continue after making such a big mistake? Or is that even a problem? We may see a visually unappealing bike lane, but it's vital to move past our assumptions to understand how the worker saw their error and then corrected it.

Assumptions are a part of every person's life. As a school counselor, it is essential to learn to identify when assumptions are creeping into our work or at least become suspicious of assumptive thinking. There are many ways to interrupt our assumptions. For example, empowering students to lead the "dance" of a counseling session leads to more fruitful outcomes for them. Providing clients with opportunities to be in charge of their counseling session by sharing essential information, also known as a *one-down* approach, validates clients and enhances their engagement. This *one-down* approach also works well to understand clients' cultural or developmental issues. When school counselors ask questions like: "What do I need to know about your family?" or "How can you help me understand your family?" it reinforces the idea that clients are the experts on themselves. Blending *one-down* position with *in-between questions* can help counselors to avoid assumptions. These questions can include "You've talked about this a lot, is this what we should focus on?" If the student says, "Yes" then the next question can be, "What are you willing to do about that issue?" or "What are you currently doing?"

Sound Bites: Things to Remember From This Section

1. We all make assumptions about our clients.
2. Recognizing when you are making an assumption and then interrupting the assumption is vital.
3. Two statements that can be used to interrupt: (A) Is this a topic you want to talk about or do something about? (B) What are you willing to do?

SECTION 9: ENHANCING CLIENT CHOICES

You cannot control the behavior of others, but you can always choose how you respond to it. —Roy T. Bennett

What Is This Section About and How Does It Connect With SFT?

It's hard to know what to do when a student comes in, talking a mile a minute about anything and everything going on in their lives. This chapter will examine how using SFT helps counselors focus on the main presenting issue for the client and enhance their choices.

A Brief Story

As a school counselor, your primary role is to help students learn. To do that most effectively, they need to be in class. Of course, we cannot provide long-term therapy because of the sheer number of clients we interact with, but we do provide therapeutic support to help clients through the day-to-day issues that they encounter. We need to let them lead and understand that we are not able to solve their issues, only clients can solve their issues. However, by letting clients lead and staying in the moment, we can provide the support they need.

When clients walk in, the first thing out of their mouth isn't always what they want to talk about. Their teacher may have sent them to us, hoping we can help them get regulated and ready to learn. Often, clients have no clear idea of what they need. What they know is that we are open to listening and supporting change. The main thing to remember is to rely on foundational listening skills. These include restating content, reflecting a feeling, and using open-ended questions along with clarifying questions like, "What would help you today," and "What do you need today to get back to class?" are always useful. We can also keep coming back to the question, "What's one thing you can do right now?" This can help a client from feeling overwhelmed or consumed and focus them on finding solutions to their issues.

Sound Bites: Things to Remember From This Section

1. It is easy to get caught up in all of the stories and issues that clients share. It's important to narrow our focus.
2. Clients may not want to talk about the thing that's really bothering them and that's okay.
3. Clients will make changes when it is the right person, at the right place, at the right time.
4. We may be that person, time, and place, or we may not be this time.

SECTION 10: RESISTANT CLIENTS

It is easier to resist at the beginning than at the end. —Leonardo Da Vinci

What Is This Section About and How Does It Connect With SFT?

This section explores the notion that clients are most ready to change when they have reached the right time, in the right place, and with the right person.

A Short Story

Clients aren't always ready to take action or find a solution. Many counseling theories would consider these clients as resistant, or opposed to therapeutic initiatives and change. As a counselor steeped in SFT, I don't believe in resistant clients. Instead, I try to remind myself that clients will change when they are ready, not when I think they are ready. Clients change when it is the right time, right place, and right person and if they seem unwilling to change, it is because they aren't ready yet. They may be ready later in the day, or tomorrow.

Rather than seeing them as resistant, I remind myself that I just don't know their dance. But I know who is in charge of that, I am. Clients need to ponder their options. When appropriate, reviewing options with them includes opportunities that have meaning for the client and then time to process which opportunity to pursue. I must be patient, give myself permission to slow down, listen, and rely on foundational skills. To understand my clients, I must rely upon them.

Sound Bites: Things to Remember From This Section

1. Remind yourself that clients change when they want to.
2. Clients are more inclined to make changes when they have options that make sense to them and are allowed time to consider those options.

SECTION 11: CONTROVERSIAL THOUGHTS— DON'T WORK HARDER THAN YOUR CLIENTS

A man can make what he wants of himself if he truly believes that he must be ready for hard work and many heartbreaks. —Thurgood Marshall

What Is This Section About and How Does It Connect With SFT?

This section, potentially one of the most controversial in this book, will review the idea that counselors should not work harder than their clients. School counselors working in SFT must embrace this mindset for a variety of reasons to best serve their clients.

A Brief Story

As a school counselor, one of the things that I have to work the hardest to remember is that I cannot work harder than my client. It is important to remember that the client is the agent of change. As a counselor, I walk alongside my clients, but I cannot force them into action, no matter how much I would like to.

When other school counselors, teachers, and administrators hear this phrase, they often recoil at the idea that we should only work as hard as the client is willing to work. It is important to delineate the idea of not working harder than your client from "don't work too hard." Counseling is incredibly demanding and we must do our very best every time we work with a client. However, it is foundational to really listen to clients and not come to the table with our own solutions ready to make them a reality. Similarly, we must always bring our "A Game" each time we meet with a client. There are many issues that clients may not want to address, despite the desires of others in their lives. As school counselors who are marinating in SFT, knowing and understanding the goals your client may or may not have is essential to finding a healthy balance between bringing your "A Game" and not working harder than your client.

A Related Short Story

A student has low grades. It is easy to assume that they want to get better grades. However, what is most important to understand is how your client perceives their low grades. Some students are okay with getting the lowest possible passing grade because they just want to graduate and don't see the point of working harder than they have to today. As a school counselor, it's important to understand the client's goal and work to support them in that area. Without this mindset, it's easy to get frustrated or burn the relationship by making the client feel like you aren't listening to them.

It is important to discuss your mindset with administrators and fellow educators to help them understand where you are coming from. In my first role as a school counselor, I often talked with my principal about how I was committed to supporting students as much as I could, but that I also wouldn't work harder than them to accomplish goals. Over time, my principal understood how this played out in practice and eventually started embracing this idea himself and would promote it with other staff. All educators can benefit from this idea because it leads to more positive mental health outcomes and less frustration.

A school counselor has to focus to ensure that they don't work harder than their client. Keeping this mindset and establishing boundaries creates the most positive outcomes for the client, as well as the school counselor. When school counselors determine to keep these boundaries, they build more effective counseling relationships, stay humble, and prevent burnout. While it may take a bit of work on the front end, this mindset is essential to remaining effective throughout a career.

Sound Bites: Things to Remember From This Section

1. Maintaining a balance is essential to developing and keeping a positive counseling relationship with your client, which is the most crucial to affecting positive change.
2. What a parent wants could be different than what the classroom teacher may want. And all of these goals might be the antithesis of what a student desires.

3. This tension is exceptionally difficult to navigate, but the client must be truly understood to work toward positive outcomes.

SECTION 12: SIX MORE BELIEFS TO HELP KEEP YOU ON TRACK

The only way to create a foundational document that could stand the test of time is to build in enough flexibility that future generations will be able to adapt it to their own needs and uses. —Diane Wood

What Is This Section About and How Does It Connect With SFT?

Six more foundational beliefs can help to guide school counselors in their work with clients.

Small Change Leads to Bigger Change

SFT is all about change. As mentioned earlier, change doesn't always mean good, it just means change, positive and negative. Sometimes we are listening for the big changes that happen to clients. The problem with this approach is that change doesn't often come in big chunks. More often, the client does one thing differently to see how it will go. That's the moment of incremental change we need to be listening for.

"That sounds different," is a statement I often make to clients. "How did that work out?" is another. I recognize the change and then ask them to explore the change.

Change in One Part of the System Leads to Chaos

While change is what we are listening for, and focusing on with our clients, we recognize that change leads to chaos, both externally and internally. For example, a middle school student who decides to cut back, not eliminate, being the class clown. Being the class clown garners attention, however, as the student begins to try out this change, there is pressure from peers, and maybe adults, who are not used to the new personality. They may be confused and unsure of how to interact with the change. Plus, some of them will be uncomfortable because they rely upon the class clown to provide support for their role. In this scenario, there will be others who will question change because they are concerned for the person changing, or for themselves.

Likewise, there is internal resistance to change. Consider any big life decision you have made. Getting into or out of a relationship, going to college, accepting a new job, moving to a new place, you get the idea. Now remind yourself of the pressure that others applied regarding these changes as well as the pressure you put on yourself. This is the internal resistance to change. It creates internal chaos that makes you question your decisions. Both of these reactions happen with clients who have a desire to make a change, but the resulting chaos makes it difficult to maintain the change.

Counselors Do Not Have the Power or Knowledge to Change Clients

Counselors are not the experts on their clients, clients are the experts on themselves. Forgetting this axiom gets counselors into trouble. The moment we forget that we need clients to help us understand them, their life experiences, their issues, their abilities, and who they are, we begin to think we are smarter about clients than they are. Counselors have foundational training and an understanding of clinical theories and beliefs about how to work with clients and what makes a difference. But equally important is the client's knowledge and life experiences.

No Two Situations Are Exactly Alike

Each client is unique and each client's situation is unique. Counselors can create problems when they assume that one client's concern is exactly like another's. They are not. Clients deserve us to bring our best listening skills into each session and to offset our assumptions about what we are hearing.

No Situation Is All Negative

Clients will present problems that seem all-encompassing in a situation where nothing is going right. However, as a solution focused counselor, it is always possible to spot the times when the problem isn't occurring and be curious about those moments. For example, when a client tells you how horrible everything is, it is important to remember that they somehow got to you. They got up, got dressed, and went out the door to school. They made it to a class or two, and then somehow they got to you. Being curious about how they accomplished all of that is important since it can help the client understand what's happening when the issue doesn't interrupt their daily activities.

Success Is Negotiable

What might seem like a successful outcome for clients may not seem like a good choice for anyone else in the world. However, clients set the pace for change. For example, a client who is passing three classes with D– grades and failing two classes may, at the moment, be perfectly content moving the two failing grades to D–. This is change. As discussed earlier, small changes are vital as they lead to bigger changes.

Sound Bites: Things to Remember From This Section

1. Keep these six issues in mind as you work with clients to better understand how to apply SFT to your work.

CHAPTER 4

NOW WHAT?

SFT Techniques

Great dancers are not great because of their technique, but because of their passion.
—Martha Graham

What Is This Section About and How Does It Connect With SFT?

The focus of this chapter is to offer some specific solution focus techniques for school counselors to use, as well as other techniques that may not necessarily be considered solution focused.

Introduction and Some Basic Reminders

Being steeped in SFT is vital to applying it consistently with your clients. Techniques are tools that support your work, but they are not the linchpin to successful work with clients. When I first began to make presentations on SFT, I spent time talking about techniques and how they connected with the theory. Then my mentor and friend Eve Lipchik wrote a book focused on understanding theory and not worrying about specific techniques. Over the years, we have continued to have this discussion and now I start my presentations with the following comment, "I don't care about techniques except that they provide a tool for me to help me understand my client. It is more important to understand the foundational beliefs and have those integrated into your work than it is to know how to ask a miracle question." I understand that this makes students and practitioners nervous. However, some of this anxiety can be laid at the foot of academic training. Professors, like myself, spend a lot of time exposing students to a variety of successful theories, often focusing on the techniques over the foundational beliefs. This approach is the opposite of how to actually apply a theory in practice. The techniques are tools, and the underlying beliefs are fundamental to applying the theory. With that in mind, should you be uncertain of the foundational beliefs, I encourage you to go back and reread sections from the previous chapters.

Slow Down and Create a Relationship

While this is not specifically a technique, it is an important consideration when using counseling techniques. Let's call it a pre-technique. Just because you know a technique, is it important to use one? Have you first fully considered the relationship that you have established? Creating a relationship with your client is the most vital component and sets the stage for working together with your client. This is why slowing down and creating a relationship yields better results for clients. More work on the front end getting to know clients leads to client success and, more importantly, clients having a sense of solving their own issues.

Miracle Question

This is a technique that is most associated with SFT. If you have studied SFT in your coursework then the miracle question may be the one thing you remember. However, without a thorough understanding of the belief system underlying SFT using the miracle question, or any technique is useless.

In general, the miracle question can set the stage to explore what change will look like for the client. For example, a counselor can begin by stating, "When you go to sleep a miracle occurs and when you wake up something is different, what is different?" I have heard many responses to this question and often the first few responses are things like getting $1 million, or a new house, or a new family. But once they buy into the question, it is important to listen closely to their responses because the client will provide some threads to the change. The miracle question not only provides information but also opportunities to be curious about what the client is interested in exploring. Filling out the picture can be accomplished by using questions like "What would I notice?" Or, you could ask, "Think of someone who knows you well. What would they notice that has changed?" This exploration can lead to more questions like, "How did you make that happen in your miracle?" "When have you done this in the past?" (again assume good intentions) and remind yourself that this isn't the first time that a client has faced adversity.

Positive Blame—Reinforce Influence in Their Own Life

My goal is to acknowledge any change by clients. When a client shares that they have made a friend using ideas that we talked about, my response is, "Wonderful news, how did YOU make that happen?" This is especially important when working with secondary clients like teachers, parents, and administrators who come to you with concerns about a student. They are worried about the student. If after you meet with the client, things begin to change, you need to be careful. This is a dangerous position because it might seem that you are the linchpin. As mentioned earlier, this scenario can mean that every student who has trouble turning in homework, or whatever the issue is, will be sent to you. However, a reframe that utilizes positive blame is to immediately ask the teacher, "How did you make that happen?" The teacher will probably be reluctant to take credit but this is your opportunity to persist and encourage them to carefully consider what they did to influence the change. Positive blame when clients do things well offers them positive support for their actions and reinforces the idea that clients play the most important role in their change.

Flag the Minefield—Prepare for Relapse

Clients slide back into previous behavior. Sometimes they head back to what they are comfortable doing. Sometimes they are checking to be sure that the change is one they wish to keep or that others will accept. Preparing your client for just such an eventuality is one of my favorite techniques. It allows the client and counselor to explore the things that are working, and recognize signs that indicate when a client begins to move back into old habits. More importantly, it recognizes solutions that clients have used previously to create change and encourages them to use them again.

Scaling Questions

This is another technique often associated with SFT. School counselors can easily adapt scaling questions at all levels. I have seen school counselors have markers on their floor with numbers, weather (sunny to stormy), and zones of regulation. When their clients come in, they can immediately go to the marker that represents where they are at this moment. This can lead to a discussion or you can ask the client where they would like to be. By using this technique, you interrupt your assumption that the client needs to move from stormy to sunny or 1 to 10. Maybe the client only needs to move to cloudy and rainy conditions or from 1 to 2? The actual number, color, or change is less important than the client's information regarding the change that has taken place or needs to take place to create change. Scaling questions do more than simply assign a number to a client's current state. Instead, they offer opportunities to examine change. As always, it is important to allow the client to lead as much as possible and rely upon their own experiences and previous successes at solving issues.

I Am Not Buying That: Caring Confrontation

This technique relates to dancing with clients. The counselor dances with the client, attempting to follow the client's lead UNTIL the client says one thing and does another. Sometimes they show one emotion but act differently. Confronting clients in a caring way can help us understand how they view their world. This is a vital approach to client work and requires that counselors become comfortable with confrontation. I often start these changes to the dance with, "I am confused by what you are saying and what you are doing. They don't seem to line up." Or "Help me to understand how that works for you when you say one thing but act in a completely different way."

Sound Bites: Things to Remember From This Chapter

Being familiar with techniques is important, however, understanding and utilizing the underlying beliefs is vital to using SFT.

CHAPTER 5

BE GILLEN

A knower may know himself. That is his limit. —Carl Gustav Jung

After completing this book, I added this chapter.

A funny thing happened while teaching an advanced graduate course on theory and skills. The focus of the training was on applying solution focused counseling beliefs to work with clients. I had a speaker talking about theory and practice with the class, so I stepped out for a few minutes and when I returned I noticed that he was wearing a new T-shirt with my face on it. While taken aback, I figured he was just giving me a hard time, but then I glanced at the students in the class and saw they all had the same shirt on. It's a classroom full of students wearing a shirt emblazoned with my face and the words, "Be Gillen. The world will adjust."

I have had similar experiences with students over the years until now without the shirts. The resulting conversation has often gone like this, "So, Dr. Gillen I heard your words in my head and then I said that to my client…" While this is gratifying as an instructor, I explain to students that I don't want them to be Gillen. You can't be me, any more than I can be you. The goal is to immerse yourself in the theory so that the beliefs are ingrained in how you think about working with clients. The goal is for you to be you and use your language with clients, not anyone else's.

Sound Bites: Things to Remember From This Chapter

1. Solution focused counseling is predicated on the clients solving their own issues and being reinforced by their actions for long-term impact.

2. While you can learn from someone with more experience and practice, in the end, you only take from them and apply the lessons learned in your own way.

ABOUT THE AUTHORS

Dr. Mark Gillen trained at the Brief Family Therapy Center and has practiced Solution Focused Therapy (SFT) since the mid-1980s. Since 2005, he has worked as a professor at the University of Wisconsin-River Falls where he trains school counselors. The focus of his work and research is the application of Solution Focused Theory with clients. He has published articles and book chapters, as well as presented at state, national, and international conferences on SFT.

Blake Mayes has been an educator for nearly a decade, first serving as a deaf/blind intervener and then as a high school counselor for the last five school years. He received his MSE in counseling from the University of Wisconsin-River Falls.